SO SPEAK THE STARS

Poetry and Prose

in the Throes of Identity Crisis

by

Tawni Waters

with illustrations

by

Desiree Wade

Also by the author:

The Long Ride Home Sourcebooks-Fire, 2017

Beauty of the Broken

Simon & Schuster, 2014

Siren Song

Burlesque Press, 2014

So Speak the Stars

Poetry and Prose in the Throes of Identity Crisis

by Tawni Waters

ISBN: 978-1-945784-09-5

©Tawni Waters 2018

Library of Congress Control Number in progress

Cover and internal images © 2018 Desiree Wade

Cover Design by Arlene Ang

Texture Press

1108 Westbrooke Terrace

Norman, OK 73072

Managing Editor: Susan Smith Nash, Ph.D.

www.texturepress.org

With Thanks:

I would like to thank by gorgeous daughter, the brilliant artist Desiree Wade, for creating the stunning illustrations that grace the cover and pages of this book. Arlene Ang for the incredible cover design. Valerie Fox for championing this work at Texture Press. Susan Smith Nash and the entire Texture team who put so much love into the creation of this collection. Grant Clauser, whose advice on constructing a poetry manuscript was invaluable. To Olivier Lebleu for making sure the French contained in these poems didn't sound like it was written by an American girl whose French was abysmal, at best (which it was). My precious momma, who survived cancer while I was writing this work. My amazing son, Timothy John Hackett, who walked away from a deadly car accident as I worked on this collection. My beloved big brother, who died of a heart attack and lived to tell the tale (thank God) as this book was being finalized. Almost losing three of the people I love most made me so grateful for all I have, including but not limited to Polyxeni Angelis, by soul sister and first reader. Carla Spataro, who took me in as Writer in Residence at Rosemont College during the creation of this work, becoming one of my dearest friends, and Beth Kephart, who inspired me to care for myself and love my words again. And always, my precious father, Timothy John Hackett, whose love still keeps me alive, decades after his death.

SO SPEAK THE STARS

For my Shining One,

the only sun

that ever burned me

warm.

I'm loving you

from the other side of the world.

CONTENTS

11. A Word About These Poems

Part 1: Black Hole

14.   Overlooked

15.   AWOL Icon: A Love Song Without Music

18.   Sex Ed

22.   Of Clichés and Collapsing Houses: A Writing
        Teacher's Lament

25.   High Art

26.   Miss USA

29.   Luster (Less)

31.   Labor Pains

33.   Imposter Star

34.   Outside the Chapel of Immaculate Conception

36.   Ruing Tuesday

38.   Scrapping the Centerfold

40.   Day of the Dead

42.   Hagseed Takes Manhattan

44.   St. Magdalene's Kintsugi

47.   Specter

48.   Outburst

51.   After the Potluck

54.   Phantom Limb Lover (A Prayer in Seven Parts)

56.   Fisher of Women

57.   Hamlet's Question

Part 2: Protostar

60.   1400 Montgomery Avenue

62.   So Speak the Stars

64.   Phoenix, Halfway to Rising

66.   What They Couldn't Steal

68.   *Fer L'amour Dur Toujours*

71.   Cave Painting (Magdalene's Mania)

73.   A Call to Arms, Written in the Ruins of an Ancient Castle Just Before the Rain

75.   Scrying

76.   Pythagorean Prayer

82.   Polyxeni's Pentecost

83.   Rewining Yoko Ono

86.   *Le Pain*

88.   A Stab at Graffiti Salvation

90.   Whitsun

92.   Secret Identity

94.   *Quand Devrait-Elle Voler ?*

Part 3: Big Bang

97.   Three Days After Apocalypse

100. Kitsched

101. Satori

103. Taken?

105. High Calling

107. The Lens

111. Parisian Kintsugi

115. Not I Do, But I Am

117. Meeting the Nameless Mother

119. *Capiche?*

122. What Magdalene Wrote in the Sand When the Mob Was Gone

124. Ohm

126. Radha's Death Bed

128. The Book of Him

130. From Magdalene to the Risen Christ, A Prelude to Ascension

132. Homecoming

134. Magdalene's Map

140. Phenomenon

142. Night Vision

144. Inanna's Imperatives

145. Beautiful Little Things

146. The Second Coming of Isis

148. The Triumph of Isis (illustration)

A Word About These Poems

In 2014, Simon & Schuster published my first novel, *Beauty of the Broken,* the culmination of a cherished dream. I thought I'd finally bought my proverbial stairway to heaven, imagining that life as I knew it would cease to exist and be replaced by magical evenings with Oprah on her yacht, drinking mimosas and listening to her wax rhapsodic about the unparalleled beauty of my prose.

I was half right. Life as I knew it did cease to exist. Through a series of uncanny coincidences, I lost everything familiar to me. As I grappled with the challenges of sudden public visibility (not quite as glamorous as it looks on paper), my personal life took a fast train to hell. Both of my children left for college. For various reasons, almost all of my close friendships imploded. My relationship with my landlord soured, and I moved out of my home. Worst of all, my relationship with the great love of my life was put on hold. I was decimated.

Rather than suss out a new permanent address, I decided to use my book advance to travel full time for a what I thought would be a year. I felt driven to discover what I was without my possessions, my relationships, my day job. Who was I when there was nothing but the stars and me? For almost five years (and counting), I've lived on the road, wandering all of the U.S., most of Europe, and much of Mexico, writing, teaching, speaking at conferences, and burrowing into self and truth.

Fate repeatedly conspired to plop me in the South of France, where legend says that one of my literary obsessions, Mary Magdalene, fled after the crucifixion of Christ. Proximity to her legend fueled my infatuation with her and all goddesses, a fascination that is reflected in these poems.

Meanwhile, back at home, a pussy-grabbing, sentient yam hijacked the presidency and did his best to rape the planet. I can't say some of my rage didn't make it to the page as well. (I wrote "Miss USA" the day he was elected.)

Every night, I whispered prayers to the only constant in my world, a sky that never changed no matter the continent, asking the stars that ridiculous question only the truly masochistic dare to ask. "Who am I really, and what is the point of all this?"

I'm not sure these writings are an answer, confused as they are, hovering somewhere between prose and poetry, but they were the only one the stars deigned to give.

Part 1:

Black Hole

Overlooked

Why does no one write the poem

about cockroaches skittering over stone

their intricate wings shimmering like polished topaz in the moonlight.

Where are
all
the odes
to
sewer rats?

What has become of the haikus written in honor of the noble earthworm?

Pink and supple he emerges from winter's white, hungry for sweet soil.

AWOL Icon: A Love Song Without Music

I vowed if I went, I'd be loving you from the other side of the world, and I airplaned away, wearing only fresh wounds and your worn out boots.

I marinated in swimming holes until brackish water raisined my fingers. I plunged under, past pirate ships and sunken plunder, kicked to the core of the earth, kissed jellyfish, liking the electric lick of their transparent tongues on my lips. I filched skeletons from coral beds, red in the light of distant underwater volcanoes. Even in the black heart of the ocean, oysters purpled and blued. The pearls in them shone like halos of Christ. And your ghost, a confused Jesus, walked under the water instead of on it. I couldn't read the book of his face, couldn't tell if he thought I was a honeyed twist of Magdalene's hair, or the hammer that drove in his nails.

I'd kiss your feet if you'd let me. I'd walk across the ocean. I'd Lazarus my love for you to life, because it was never dead anyway, not even sleeping. I suffocate it between my palms at night, pinch its nostrils, leave it for dead. The next day, it's exploding my head again, emerging from its grave, its shroud a cloud that settles over my eyes until all I see is white.

Thunder breaks something, and it's not just the sky.

I said if I left, when I died, I'd wait on the other side for you. Death doesn't scare me now. I dream river bottoms, soggy with longing and won't-flinch vows. I dream your eyes. I dream red flowers shuddering cold in the fist of winter. I dream you didn't mean the things you said. I dream you wish my love for you un-dead. I dream knives. I dream fire. I dream my toes trembling on a circus wire. I dream myself falling, and I don't care much. My skin doesn't pink. My heart doesn't wing. My mouth won't scream.

I used to know the taste of crimson. I used to sweat the smell of light. I could have divided every molecule by a million miracles, laid them out on the table two-by-two, amoebas entering the ark of a strip of bark, or making a raft of a dollop of grass in a glassy puddle. Now I measure my life like this: _____ days until I die.

Last night, dream me wondered why you were watching. "I'm loving you from the other side of the world," you said. I took your blessed head in my hands, pulled the thorns from your graying hair, wound dandelions between your toes, anointed your skin with holy water, made your kneecaps into altars to Mary.

We are growing old. I see my wrinkles in the mirror of your face. There is a place just to the left of my ribcage where I dug a hole and I buried every word you ever whispered. I have memorized the whorls of your fingertips. My lips have traced and tasted every bump of your tongue. Still, your name to me sounds like yellow. Still, I keep the faith. Still, I testify: the only amazing grace I ever knew was sewn like lace around the edges of your teeth.

There was never an inch of your secret sins that weren't mine times ten.

There was never a scrap of your sacred skin I didn't know how to love.

Sex Ed

Little girl, they said your name the way
the once-rich homeless man asked the college kid for food
managing to sound hungry and condescending at once.
The way the water bug seemed
to be showing off when he defied physics.

The rules are for you and not for me.

The way the lies poured from politicians' mouths
like concrete solidifying around the truth
until there was nothing left
but mounds of something unidentifiable
and definitely terrifying.

(We would never find out.)

Let it be known that the day you gave
your blessed virginity away
the sun exploded, spattering
orange chaos over the horizon
as he, utterly unworthy, grunted
for a thousand years
or perhaps briefly

depending on how drunk you were.

(Alternatively, your deflowering
lasted as long as a May fly's forever,
and you never made a sound.)

Before the dawn, you woke
to find your sheets stained with blood
and weeping, you watched
the moon curl itself
like a toenail over the crest
of the mountain, whispering,

"Hush now. Your rivers
still run downhill,
and isn't that enough?"

When your waters dried up
you sensed a goddess
in the spaces between electrons
and thought that if you learned her name
she might take your cessation
an offering
and call you by the name
of love.

That very night, in the sight
of six invisible witnesses
you touched yourself
as if God wasn't watching
as if the stars didn't whisper

the secret to everything.

The shamelessly flagrant red flowers
your father called Indian paintbrushes
dipped themselves in mud
and wrote on the sky
printing in careful calligraphy
Patsy Clyne's name
three times in white
with the phrase

stand by your man

etched in the stones below.
stammering, stilted, but still slotted
with fool's gold
or iron pyrite, as the nuns called it
loathe to speak the common
names of sacred things.

Woman, who knew
when you read those words
that after all that you'd been through
you would receive them as truth
spread wide your maiden maw
swallow them whole
shells and all

never stopping
to question
the whys?

Of Clichés and Collapsing Houses:
A Lovelorn Writing Teacher's Lament

I teach my students to choose their details carefully. Don't tell us everything, I instruct them. Give readers telling details, through which they can construct the whole in their imaginations. But I cannot verbally reproduce the parts of you that would make it possible for anyone to construct the whole in all its glory. Three parts lightning, three parts blue jeans, four parts God. Is that what I should write? Should I say something about the fire in your eyes, or is that cliché? That is really the telling detail, if ever there was one. But to paint it, I'd need actual matches, maybe some lighter fluid. And even when you were there in person, no one seemed to notice but me.

Should I mention the dent in your throat?

Are they blind?

I teach too about load bearing scenes. Make the moments that matter *matter*, I tell them. Give them space on the page. They have to carry a lot of weight. If they aren't strong enough, the whole house will collapse. But how do I tell them that my entire life hangs on one split second, when:

I saw you standing under a night reeling with stars, and my molecules reconfigured themselves? In an instant, every cell in my body flew to you, the way metal filings fling themselves at a magnet.

And here, I am defying the laws of physics while mixing architecture and science metaphors.

Should I even be allowed to teach?

And then I go all Clint Eastwood on them. I tell them to loosen up on the reigns, let their imaginations ride like palominos through the deserts of their psyches, but when I let my horses run free, they always run to you, and what does that say about me and my artistry? I am a one note piano, a lone trick circus monkey, a yellow bird that sings the same song again and again.

You told me my cage was in my head, so I bent the bars until they broke.

You untethered me from this world, if we might draw upon a playground metaphor now. You know that white ball on the string the mean kids bounce around and around? I was that until you found me and cut my rope. Before I broke through to the other side of the atmosphere, my journey was a mother fucker. Now it's just me and the stars.

It is quiet here. I am not happy, but I am at peace. I am not alive, but I am not tortured. I am alone, but I am not lonely.

Some days, I wish I would fly straight into the face of the sun.

High Art

I met Mona Lisa and was unimpressed.

This little square of dazzle-less paint drowning

in a sea of sweating bodies, hungry to be seen and see,

to check "Mona Lisa and me" off their selfie bucket list.

The last thing I felt was inspired. You want enigmatic,

give me the way the sun melts low over the horizon,

oozing heaven all around, even though tonight,

people will die because it's dark. Women will be raped

in alleys after a mesmerizing sunset, and that's a kind of art

whose message you can't quite pin down. You want mystery,

look at how the magnificent sea rolls, being judgement day,

ready to suck us all under and feed us, along with piles

of ancient pirate plunder, to the sharks. Who decided

what was art? Who said I had to be more moved

by the Mona Lisa than by subway graffiti created

by my cousin Ralph? The greatest painting

I ever saw lived in the eyes of a small-time musician.

He smiled, and I saw God.

Miss USA

Here is a cardboard crown. Dub yourself queen of the trailer park. It's all yours. The lawn chairs, the pink flamingos, the entire six-pack of Pabst Blue Ribbons.

A parade of singlewides marches this way, 666 miles long, and every inch of warped paneling belongs to you. Overflowing ashtrays upend themselves in your presence. Coke can bongs genuflect. As you pass, dumpsters gape, agog in the smog, begging for a morsel from your hand, a moment to stand basking in the flickering florescent light of your eyes, a chance to say, "I saw her, I bought her, she was on sale at WalMart today for 19.99."

The VIP swine in the pen behind the rec room snort your name ad nauseum. When you swing open the door to your double wide, the fat man on the stoop smooths his wife beater, slicks back his six strands of hair. "She's coming," he whispers. "The queen of cool kids and kitsch." He switches on the bug zapper to impress you. A tiny bolt of lightning brings sudden death to a passing beetle.

That's how powerful you are. Electricity follows you wherever you go. In the dive bar down the street, neon signs flicker when you settle in to watch Maury on the big screen. Big hair cover bands massacre Warrant songs in your honor. Sweet cherry pie, you have backstage passes. You smoke pot on the urine-scented couch, take selfies with meth infested roadies, sort the front row fans yourself.

At the flea market, you set up your shelves, spread out your mass-produced mundanity. Flat earth proponents fist fight for the chance to sample your wares. You curled your thinning hair for this, spread lipstick over your lipless, skeletal grin, and they notice. A reverse messiah, you turned wine into water. They guzzle it by the gallon, drink themselves blind, sacrifice their miniscule minds on your altar of mediocrity.

Their Jesus came wrapped in a flag packaged with a semi-automatic and a complimentary bag of bullets, saying,

"Blessed are the peacemakers, and by peacemakers, I mean hypocrites, warmongers, and genocidal imperialists."

Just this morning, they passed a moratorium on reading, but they still appreciate art. A sacred heart made of beer tabs hangs in the office, next to a calendar from the year 1956. A velvet Elvis looks on. His oil paint eyes are wrong, but he smiles just the same. You are just the girl he's been waiting for.

You've made it, darlin'.

You're really something.

The whole trailer park knows your name.

Luster (Less)

Don't you feel gray inside,

organs   bags of grainy sand

skin   stripped bare

of everything   that made you shine?

Your options for rock bottom

have multiplied   exponentially.

Heroin addiction   is a best case scenario.

Time has always been   a steel jawed trap,

and now its teeth

are

        closing

            tight.

Last night, there was

        a hole

            in my dreams

                where you

                used to stand

            a torrential up pour

of quick sand.

Bad whiskey tastes sick sweet

like   forgetting

and that's enough to make me

                  suck

            it

down.

I wonder if this pain

camouflages   the real me

like flat black spray paint   on a cherry red corvette

or if underneath   I was always

                  this color

            of

dead.

Labor Pains

I hid you in my womb, and it was not enough.
Not close enough, not safe enough.
When you love something best, you bury it
in your flesh, right in the middle, where no one
can find it, but I couldn't keep you there,
and when you left my body

your hair was the color of house finches' eggs,
speckled blond. I didn't love you, exactly,
because love is trite and small and fits handily
on Hallmark card. What I felt for you
was an atomic bomb. It exploded me.
Shockwaves ripple even now, 23 years later
and last year, when you called to tell of metal

meeting motorcycle, painted a picture of you curled
in a fetal position just the way you slept inside me,
only this time, you were on a sidewalk, watching
that man who'd T-boned you bleed out, I wanted
to take you and bury you in me again,
in the safest place, where nothing could ever touch you,
but all I could do was listen to you wail.

No newsflash, no crime, no war, no genocide
had ever managed to make me hate this world,
but when life broke you, the mother beast
in me wanted to make a mess of this planet,
rip it from limb to limb, strew sinew and skin
over distant moons bellowing.

I drove to you and touched your face,
the same face that blinked up at me
after my traitorous womb evicted you,
without permission. You just came,
and there you were, breathing, being miraculous,
and something bigger than love exploded.

Your fingers were so small,
and the world was so big.
I understood the meaning of fear.

Imposter Star

People say I'm rising.

Every time they clap, line up, ask me to write my name, I remember this plastic bag I saw blowing across the park back in New York when you and I missed one another by a minute. Remember? I waited for you all day in a café, watching out a window, terrified you might pass and somehow, I wouldn't see.

At night I think back, wonder if I jinxed us by being scared, or if I let the devil in when out of kindness, I turned to speak to that man who wouldn't leave me be. I never saw you, just that red bag, and thought it was like me without you, beautiful to look at, ethereal even, soaring, riding breezes, carefree, but heading nowhere fast, or worse, somewhere--an iron gate, a gutter, a sharpened picket fence.

It was inflated, full of wind, crammed with everything that doesn't matter, pregnant with nothing. I watched that hollow thing dance until it was a red speck on the horizon. It could have been the morning star, but I knew that it wasn't.

It was a bit of trash, a jot of mundanity, an empty thing playing at being spectacular.

Outside the Chapel of Immaculate Conception

Above the church, a stone Mary stands guard,
her marble flesh spit-shined by rain and moon.
Jewel-backed beetles skitter over stone walls.
Sane seekers have long since slinked home
breath wine red, tainted with wafers
blood washed white, absolved of sin.
I breathe out. She breathes in.
Granite eyes peer beneath my skin.

Blighted by a thousand invisible birthmarks,
I wear a map to heaven on my back.
At night, constellations swirl to life
between my shoulder blades.
Having been evicted from my forehead,
my third eye sits squarely at the nape of my neck

a lesion
a tumor
a curse.

But it is not that.

My sight is a flower I can never wear in my hair.
She understands, having watched
weeping as a thousand witches screamed,
the blossoms of their burning flesh blooming
orange, staining sky with soot.

The stone Mary has a heart. At night,
she stands wailing, throttled by starlight,
weaving garlands of honeysuckle
between cold, gray fingers. Snowflakes graze
her cheeks like moth wings. Melting, they seep
into her grooves, turn to ice

make her crack.

Ruing Tuesday

If my courage had not turned in on itself
if I had not stabbed out the moon's one yellow eye
if I had not counted the red stones
as cherries, and swallowed them
I would have found a way to undo my dressing
come to you naked, without socks, free of my stilettos.
I would have never fallen down those stairs.
You would not have found me crumpled like that,
mistaken me for a pile of dirty laundry.
If you had spoken more clearly
if your tongue had not spiraled as it did
I would never have thought of a corkscrew
when I looked at you. I would not have kept
my belly button close, fearful of its unraveling.
And what of the wind? What part does she play in this?
We could argue that had she not gathered the leaves
in bunches and cast them into the sewers' throats
the alligators never would have been coughed up
having grown hulking and enraged, thrashing,
seeking vengeance for their flushings. We know
if the toilet had not overflowed that night, the living fish
that Billy tried to bury at sea might have made it to the river,
no longer a goldfish, but a dazzling, gargantuan, carpy thing.

He would have swum upstream, convinced

some scantily clad salmon he was just the mate

she'd been looking for. Had he soaked her eggs

in his sperm, we might have known the wonder

of rose hued goldfish. Our aquariums would run over

with miracles. But now, we have only this:

these four gray pebbles that fell from your pocket

as you went, and those shoes you left by the front door

untied and gaping, longing for the shape

of your feet.

Scrapping the Centerfold

Honey, what did you think would happen?
You have learned the hard way the cost
of being a man's dirty little secret, what it means
to be the flesh and bone equivalent of the stack
of *Playboys* under his high school bed. He pulls
you to him when the moon is full, inspects
your intricacies with his flashlight, lets you lick
his trembling fingers, see a side of him
no one else knows. But when the sun comes up,
into the box you go. It's dark. A layer of dust
covers you, coats your nose, your tongue,
your throat, the pink insides of your lungs.
You cough black ooze when you cum.
Is it cancer? No one cares, least of all him.

Girl, stop me if you've heard this one. When his mom
finds you and goes batshit, he cries for a time,
but he doesn't stand in her way. You end up
in the alley dumpster, beside last week's chicken salad
and Sunday paper. Next morning, he and his sweetie
ride by on their bikes. Your negligee-laced pages,
now stained with coffee, flutter in the breeze.
He's already forgotten your fading nipples,

the way that dog-eared edge
made your one eye seem off.

Sister, pipe down, and take it like a woman.
That warmth you felt at the Circle-K the day
he shoved you under his jacket meant nothing.
You were already trash-in-the-making.

Kid, don't say I didn't warn you.
When the garbage truck rumbles up the street,
he won't even glance your way.

Day of the Dead

Corpses howl in the streets, clacking corroded teeth, and I should be scared, but I'm not. I weave them marigold crowns, lie down among headstones, summon spirits to talk. We know secrets, we dead things. The only difference between me and them is I still have my skin. Three tokes in because the only time I feel alive is when I'm high enough to hallucinate you. They say I'm living the dream, but fame was never my dream. My dream was me curled into the question mark of your body like an answer.

There is no rage left. Just my insides rattling around like shattered glass. Just the sucking sound my rib cage makes 24/7, reminding me it's empty.

Today, I ran until my lungs almost exploded. While my heart clobbered my chest, I fell in the grass and looked up. Heaven was broken, slit into strips of gray and white. The air trembled. Night was coming, and the sky knew it. I slept and dreamed I was Lazarus, wrapping those clouds around me like bandages. You were Jesus outside the tomb, saying, "Come forth!" And I came, your blessed name on my lips.

You are Jesus, so build me a ladder to heaven.

You are Jesus, so build me a stairway to your face.

I will climb it, crawl into the amazing grace of your
mouth, and sleep there, warm on the mattress of your tongue,
my head propped on the pillows of your teeth.

The moon coats tombstones in white.

Stars slop light everywhere, and who cares?

You were the only sun that ever burned me warm.

Hagseed Takes Manhattan

She was a woman given to pageantry, though she shouldn't have been, looking as she did like overripe fruit left to wither in a casing of sequins.

It wasn't her face that made her ugly. (I'll admit it didn't help.) It was her soul, which hunched like twin raisins, scrunched and desiccated, at the center of her eyes. She eviscerated bad baristas, sighed only in French, said her prayers in pig-Latin backwards, and kept a brown bag full of Etruscan cigarettes by her bed. Her head was badly misshapen from longing for a crown, the down above her lip stained red from blood oranges and a coarse and strident longing she could never fill.

What she needed was a reverse-will, her mother bequeathing her something other than extra chins and a worn-out disco ball. Maybe a hall for beheading peasants, an unexploded hand grenade, tangerine marmalade, jade green eyes, any kind of talent, a pair of thighs that didn't touch, a hutch chocked full of white rabbits fresh from the magician's hat, Joe DiMaggio's baseball bat, a good girdle, a swimming pool brimming with raspberry Jell-O and the secrets of sexual desire.

She aspired to become a movie star, draping herself over every cherry red car she saw, taking deep draws from her long, long cigarette, Cruella De Vil style. And oh, that smile. Watch out Pennywise, you've met your match.

Some Julys, she put on shows, rose to greet her fans, her pudgy hand haughtily extended. "You may kiss the royal rings." And her German shepherds would. She wasn't just good, she was *real* good. The neighborhood went wild!

Encore! encore! You're a star!

Crowbar your way into the limelight!

How upsetting! How bizarre!

What exactly is she *doing* to that poor, poor cherry red car?

Who needs talent? You just need money (and they have Kickstarter for that).

Pass the hat. Sign autographs.

Keep out the riffraff. Scourge the wait staff.

(And laugh--don't ever forget to laugh.)

Flash that Cheshire grin. Tuck in your six chins.

Straighten your cardboard crown.

Paint the Big Apple a fine shade brown.

Let out your gently used Marilyn Monroe gown, and rock it, babe. Walk that rented red carpet. Sure, you're slightly dented. You've been around the block a time or ten, but please believe me when I tell you, my glamorous, mysterious misery maven, you don't look a day over 66.

Ok. Maybe 67.

St. Magdalene's Kintsugi

"Even after all this time, the sun never says to the earth, You owe me. Look what happens with a love like that. It lights up the whole sky." Hafiz

They lied when they said she came to his feet with a year worth of wages tucked neatly into her little jar, gold turned to oil and poured over his head, a costly gift that said "I love you" in precisely the right way to make him smile, forgive her sins, write in the sand with a slow, sacred hand, stop that mob from throwing stones.

Sometimes the truth is too big to stuff into a story. Only so much treasure can be alchemized to words. How do you say:

She came with everything. Decades worth of wages. Every page of her book. The women she might have been. The other lives she willingly traded to become the prophecy's hated whore. Her youth and

the years the years the years the years the years

she could have given to children. How can an alphabet of consonants capture the howling of her babies in their beds while his holy head was anointed? You need raw, open vowels to say the jar was her only heart, and it cracked, one of those

Japanese containers that never gets made new and beautiful by fissures of gold.

And when the mob dragged her to the street, he was the man who had been sleeping in her bed, but he said nothing, just stood there, letting them lob their rocks while she knelt in the sand screaming, his silence breaking her more than any stone ever could.

She looked up to the sky, wondering when praying not to die turned to praying the stones would become boulders, because slow death by way of small blunt cruelties heaped on a head day after day is its own kind of brutal anointing, and she, a lesser god now, was ready to ascend to her heaven on her ladder no one could see.

Behind her curtain of whore hair slept the soul of a saint who always understood that it was a trade, her essential oils for these stones. She was a seer who knew she was a symbol too big for a story told by clumsy, dumb men who wrote her as a slut because they couldn't find the right words to say she was a human sacrifice who laid

everything everything everything everything

at his feet. She knew it would be this way, saw the mob and their rocks in her visions. "You might die for this," the angel Gabriel said when he flew in to offer the bargain, bleeding a thousand days. "A sword shall pierce your heart, but you will see god."

And Mary's soul was broad and full of flowers, Eve's hunger in reverse, Eden's endless garden, vomiting her red for a dying world. She loved her Christ the way the sea loves the sky, kisses it until it turns turquoise too, swallows heaven's hue whole, forgetting what color it was before. No one ever knew the way the ocean bled red to be blue. She said:

Yes yes yes yes yes yes yes yes yes yes yes yes

All the angel promised came to be. Mary saw god, but god couldn't see her back. Decades after the first rock flew, she sprawled there bleeding, still miraculously-but-barely breathing, her hardly-there heartbeat still a song screaming his name. The mob had turned stoning her into a national sport, a game made science by time.

Her crime of loving too much was such that she forgot her name, became just another whore dreaming of heaven under a pile of rocks, her own kind of Prometheus, crucified every day for two thousand years, old now, but still beautiful somehow, her fissures made pretty by blood, blue wounds still weeping freely, but secretly needing her forever stoning

to stop.

Specter

I wake in the night to the sound
of your disembodied voice
knocking on my skull.
I fling myself open like matching doors
carved from river wood, drawn up whole
already painted blue, cracking. I slept
in the gap between your tongue and teeth
for three whole weeks before you noticed me there
nesting like a small rodent or medium-sized bird.
You spat me out with that pat-too-ee sound
only you can make. The ground quaked
your revulsion. Sleepless, I stare into the not-yet
dawn, listening to your ghost wail, threading my fingers
through his not-there hair, kissing his invisible lips,
tasting rotting citrus and heavy air, whispering
there there there there there there there there
hoping he understands, even now,
in the wake of the tsunami of you,
the decimated island of me craves your holy water.
That Innana corpse you made of me
and hung up on your wall
has loved you all along.

Outburst

Above the steeple, sky slits her wrists, slashes lightning bolt veins until they bleed acid rain.

The chapel shudders, cinched tight in a crackling casing of kinetic energy and original sin. Gutters run red with communion wine. A stone Mary shakes her head, wondering at the mess. Clicking his honeyed tongue, Jesus thrusts out his sacred chest until his heart shows gold. Dogwood roots uncoil, soak sun from soil that hast not yet cooled, has not bothered to understand that this storm means business, is here to drive out all warmth, make refugees of rat families, drown entire ant populations in collapsing tunnels.

Remember how in the Bible they said heaven cracked? It was like that, only passing alley cats found no ark. For them, there was no Noah offering gopher wood salvation. Dripping, they bolted beneath staircases, twitching tails, howling. Hens tottered, beaks gaping wide, cursing God in six languages, aghast at their drenched, dented feathers. Squirrels stood on hind legs to pen heaven a strongly worded memo written in the alphabet of snails, sentences looking something like the slick left behind by a terrier's tongue on drywall, slippery and bumpy.

I wanted it to be like this, prayed for the sky to be angry, like me. I needed the wet to mean business, to make a damp tramp of the whole world, turn her saucy sweat to mud, drown her horrid history in the irascible sounds of thunder and the silent screams of dying sidewalk worms.

As if memory can be undone.

Once, I tried to un-carve your name from the elm where I wrote it, but it had sunk deep into the heart of the tree, become a piece of its spine. "Mine," the hungry trunk said, and swallowed your name whole. I can't say that I blame it. When I was young, I wrote your name in lipstick on bathroom walls, thick, red scrawls bleeding my love onto every surface I touched.

How can you say so much in two syllables?

Rain washes present tense away, erases the shaky line I walk between invisibility and quasi-fame. Near-acclaim, like near-beer. A tenth of the flavor, none of the kick in the head.

Once the T.V. show host asked me what my favorite word was. I said your name. She wasn't impressed. Didn't she understand the miracle of you, that there is this man who stands taller the sun and wears rainbows in his hair?

I suppose she'd have to see you to get it, the same way the word "ocean" doesn't do justice to the ever-swelling miracle of Pacific sand-sea-tide. "There are whales down there," I told her, trying to explain. "He holds whole schools of fish in his kneecaps."

The earth burps at heaven, shrugs, unmoved by her tantrum. Sky slams her door. Grassy ground says, "Come out again when you are ready to act like a lady."

The storm rolls bone white and cold over the horizon, disappearing two inches at a time, like you. I tried to hold on, but when was the last time lightning let anyone ride him bareback?

Sky emerges at dawn, dressed in pink gauze, wearing lilacs in her hair. Her singing sounds like the cardinals who gather on the steeple's point, drops of blood on a needle poking heaven's eye.

Sky doesn't cry this morning.

I huddle here beneath my upended umbrella, utterly undone.

After the Potluck

My brother, the preacher, confided that today when he was praying he told God that he hates people. "I mean me too," he added, because even in the throes of his crisis of faith, he is driven to be fair, an equal opportunity loather.

I couldn't blame him. Every day, for 30 years, he gave everything to love his flock, and when the time came for him to need them, his sheep did more than scatter. They yanked shanks from their wool and

    cut

        him

           down.

"We are God's worst creation," he said, staring at his big, cracked hands which had baptized and married and buried and ministered to the poor, the sick, the dying, the mongrels begging, always begging, for

    more

        more

           more.

My brother has permanent scars in his arms from giving blood, and when I spell it out like that, it becomes a symbol for everything he is. Even in his brokenness, he is the best man I have ever known. I wanted to hold him, say something to wash the disillusionment away, but the only counter argument I could muster was the little boy in the corner, reading a Bible with wide eyes.

He was autistic, and he commented wryly from time to time, jokes no one heard. A mop of hair obscured his eyes, and when he stood to get a drink, his feet turned in a little, pigeon toed maybe, but I thought he looked more like a penguin, one of those noble ones in the movie narrated by Morgan Freeman. He seemed like the kind of being who would brave ice and wind to return to his kin with fish, the kind who would sacrifice anything to offer sustenance. He seemed like he could love without asking for anything in return except for maybe a laugh from time to time

a smile

a cookie

a cup of cool water.

I didn't get his name, but I'll always love that kid. He saved the world for me.

I remember my brother best when he was nine wailing over the carcass of a lizard he had killed accidentally with a stray bouncing ball. He looked so small, sobbing, his shoulders shuddering. I wanted to make the world better for him, a place without brutality and decay.

Inside, my brother is still crying over the little, shattered things. Like the boy with the penguin toes, his sin is this: He doesn't hate people.

He loves them

        too

          much.

Phantom Limb Lover: A Prayer in Seven Parts

1. My life is all the colors of a full gumball machine, and still, I miss you. Beaches blister, rippling in rising day, perfect save that one spot where you should be standing, un-breaking in the waves, grabbing fistfuls of sunlight and weaving them through your hair. Seagulls scream your name. Osprey eggs rattle, cracking wide to reveal shards of your shattered eyes.

2. You are the dream I can't un-see, the song I will never un-learn. I don't want to. I chant your name five times a day, bowing toward Mecca, my rug woven from memories of your beard, my prayers cobbled from fragments of your body. He had teeth like stars. His knuckles were mountains. He wore a scar on his chin. My toes, threading their way along the thin line separating sea from sand, have memorized your footprints by heart. Even when you are invisible, I follow you. You are every hallelujah I ever sang.

3. Sun splatters sea in streams of red. I ricochet back to my moon-scented bed to taste the tongue of your memory. I recite the scriptures of your teeth. Your quicksand eyes swallow me. My brain becomes a hive of buzzing bees, blessing blossoming trees in the courtyard of an ancient temple ruin.

4. For three seconds, I finally understand Jesus, cradle him in cupped hands until he melts into rain, strains through my fingers in streams of light, puddles around my feet, the pool of him reflecting star-bloom until he monsoons to the window.

He takes his leave, dragging with him a plate of communion wafers and six full cans of beer.

5. I thrash here in the valley bisecting life and death, chained between breath and breathlessness, and when you come to me a skeleton, I learn to love your bones. I am no Buddha, but I am something. Already, I have the belly and the laugh. I hover halfway to heaven. My faith won't move mountains, but it makes messes of termite mounds. If I haven't found God, I've at least got some pretty good leads. At night, the flesh between my shoulder blades shreds to make way for embryonic wings.

6. Beloved, your grave is empty. I float in the mouth of the cave.

7. Wait for me. I'm coming.

Fisher of Women

You caught the Christ in me and scaled her,
tore her down to fishbones. She bleeds red
in your net oozing light and visions, a gaping,
witching wound, gasping for cauterization.

You caught the Christ in me and threw her
back in the River Styx. She had no death wish,
but you granted it anyway. Now, knowing
that all thoughts are prayers waiting to be answered,
all songs are hymns, all sentences are spells,
she stares silently, entombed in stinking mud.

You caught the Christ in me. Casting smooth
stones aside, with fins long dormant, she breaks
free and swims for a warped sky that looms

just above her water, slit by sunlight

sliced by a dream of heaven.

Hamlet's Question

We answer it with "not to be," losing our lives in screens, pixilated dreams set on never-ending cycles of "being is not enough," but outside our darkened windows, purple flowers pulse in rocky pockets of hillsides, insisting on being in spite of our blindness, not needing to be seen in order generate pseudo-self-esteem, esteeming what is to be more than enough.

As if your one sacred life could ever be outdone by the photoshopped, calculated sheen of a perfume ad. As if there was ever a meme that captured even a fraction of the awe inspired by the face of the moon reflected, shattered and splintered, in a moaning mirror of sea. As if the echoes of ancient stars, finally reaching our eyes after eons of travel through the watery, warped web of space-time, could ever be eclipsed by the fleeting, bleached smile of an already decaying celebrity.

Truth crashes all around you, in the molecules of air springing toward sun as you exhale, in the pebble that clattered down stone steps when you kicked it, in the water that lapped over your skin while you bathed. You closed your eyes, went under, opened your perfect mouth, drank it down, let it boil in your sacred, starving belly.

You are hungry. Step away from the dead dream screen. Life waits for you.

Swallow it whole.

Part 2:

Protostar

This is the miracle tree in which I have built my nest for now.

I sleep here, absorbing stars, drinking moonlight.

My thighs talk in tongues.

My toes telegraph messages to the universe.

who answers back

in the language of crickets and punk rock boys.

They listen to rap outside my window, smoking cigarettes and saying,

"Come here, honey.

Can't you see? You don't wanna miss this.

Our orange hair is on fire."

So Speak the Stars

So my darling, resplendent, earth shattering, miraculous thing, they said you weren't good enough. Your body wasn't the right kind of sexy and your face was wrong and your brain, well, holy shit, your brain, always coloring outside the lines, always thinking things best left unthought.

Freedom. Escape the maze. Run. Run. Run.

What if your brain is the rightest thing about you? What if it makes waves because in its holy animal core, it knows there is something more than this bullshit? What if you are such a wonder, the miracle of you couldn't be silenced, even with a billion voices trying to shout you down? What if you are perfect and pretty and none of them could ever give you the love you are looking for because it was inside you all along? What if that thing shuddering along the exquisite folds of your brain is a god that is bigger than the box they tried to shove you in to die? What if angels are singing 24/7, trying to get your attention, trying to recover their long lost love? You.

And if you're thinking this shit they keep spoon feeding you isn't enough, maybe you are onto something. What if you were born for more? And if you are miserable say so, and do something about it. Something shocking. Something irreverent and sacred all at once. Something that will bring you to your knees. Break your cage. There is such a thing as rage that shatters the machine. It's not just a band name, and you are not a brand name. There is more God in one strand of your sacred DNA than in all the churches in the world. You are a walking miracle, and fuck them all if they are too blind to see it. What matters is that you see it.

The worst they can do is kill you, and so what? Look me in the eye and tell me you truly believe that shiny thing that lives inside you is ever going to die.

Phoenix, Halfway to Rising

We thought we hated winter until the year the blizzards would not come. Longing for the storm of you, I stared at the slate of the snowless sky, knowing that death by you would be like death by freezing. It would hurt at first, but then, warmth would creep along my skin, wreathing my limbs in purple frostbite blooms. I would become a garden of lilacs, and die, melting into your eyes, thinking thank yous.

When your fire started to burn in my toes, I tried to turn my mind into a tourniquet, strangle the limbs that loved you. But I could not suffocate my own heart, so I let flames wash over me in waves, forging faith in an inferno that scorched me down to bones.

And so now, the snake of me unlocks her jaws, lets the raw meat of a moonless night slide down her throat. And so now, I make my knees into mouths that kiss the ground of your grave, and I say to the sky, "I will die here. No life without him." And so now, I smear my skin with mud and wait for your ghost to find me.

Beaked, un-feathered things shred my skin, untether me from this realm. As if death could turn these bones of steel to dust. They may rust in the rain of you, but the skeleton of this love will shimmer in the sun, long after earth is gone.

Tonight, I saw a swan, swimming in a star pricked pool, singing. Her white wings yawned wide, swallowing the night, the streetlights reflected in a rippling slick of water.

She said she couldn't die.

She said she'd gobbled the stone of you.

She said she burned to bits in the fire of your eyes and found everlasting life.

Let her make a trampoline of the moon, a ladder of the stars.

Let her weave a magic carpet from strands of your hair.

Let her rise to God.

What They Couldn't Steal

They have made a ruin of our temple.
They have slaughtered 777 sacred cows
and ground them into meat.
They set up tents in parks, pass out Pabst Blue Ribbon,
serve up blasphemy burgers with sour sides
of pickles and lies. "Do you want facts fried with that?"
they ask, and the grave diggers shriek, "Yes."
Save us Mother, for they are sin.
Our Lady of Perpetual Profanity has crowned herself queen,
shined up her six chins with glitter, whitened her fangs,
slapped a coat of forbidden fruit gloss
on her lipless, skeletal grin. She slides white tights
over cellulite, strives to compete with the moon,
rule over the night. She has hijacked the Christ,
forced him to wear her ring, put a pistol to his head,
said, "Sing my praises or else." In a fit
of self-aggrandizement, lo, our much un-beloved
psycho king shelves sanity. His Trailer Trash Brigade
reigns supreme. "Get a rope," they howl, and lynch
the goddess in the street. Some days
I think they have murdered everything that mattered,
but then I remember you, dancing under moonlight,
outshining the stars. What they couldn't steal was your heart
between my hands, pounding out its secrets,
and how I listened, memorized them word by word,
studied the spaces, the things you couldn't say.
What they couldn't steal was that day
you stood 5 feet away and said "I love you" with your eyes,
and no one knew, no one would ever know our secret,
but for those 55 seconds, no one knowing was ok.

What they couldn't steal was the miracles,
the way we morph one another's mundanity into magic,
how you walk each night on the water of my mind,
stilling waves. When days are dark, and sharks circle,
I remember the way the asphalt rippled
as you stood on it. Like me, it longed for nothing
more than to melt into your skin.
Next time around, I will come back as a swirl
on your thumb, a bump on your tongue, a white
crescent moon rising at the tip of your toenail.
This time around, I am one giant foot, shod
with the preparation of the Gospel of Your Throat.
You have un-Judas-ed me. You have de-Delilah-ed
my mind. You have redefined the whore in me as Madonna.
You made art of my heart, Sistine-Chapel-ed my soul.
My DNA sings your praises. My toes have become
New Testaments. My very elbows reek of God.

Fer L'amour Dur Toujours

In France, the cacophony of a foreign tongue settled in my ears until it became un-strange, and I began to collect words like shiny pebbles.

Coeur. Heart.

Divin. Divine.

Œil. Eye.

Os. Bone.

I built a body from sounds until you stood before me whole, each sacred shred labeled in a language born to epitomize beauty.

"Faire que l'amour dure toujours," scrawled on the wall outside my house. *The iron of love lasts forever.*

I knew it was true. Here in this village of stones, overrun by lilacs, built on the bones of centuries, they do not say, "We have had a relationship." They say, "We have a story." *Nous avons une histoire.*

Under the arched back of an ancient bridge, a river runs. Herons walk on water. I watch them, tracking our story back to the banks of a blue-green stream where we first sprang like lotus flowers, our hands clasped, a single lifeline stretched across two palms, winding around and down our wrists, up our arms, into our hearts, to the time when we slept as one in the womb-mind of the universe until the zygote of us divided, became two.

Deux fleurs divines.

You are a continent away, and still, when you weep in my dreams, it wrecks me, infects me with a horror that lasts all day, my hands grasping empty air, aching to hold you until our crying quiets and dies.

Until death do us un-part your eyes are my tunnels of light, gateways to a God who lived long before empires thought to rename her and claim her, a God who wrote her signature in a book composed in the elegant language of dark matter and DNA, a God who does not play by our petty rules but wanders wide beyond our sky, leaving footprints.

Constellations.

Supernovas.

Big bangs.

Atoms breaking, exploding into brilliant mushroom clouds of doom, then wrestling to bond, wind back down, become one again.

(And without the apocalypse of separation, could we ever have stories?)

This place has embraced me, made me its honored guest. Each night, I drink wine on terraces and flower strewn rooftops that aren't mine, laughing with friends, gazing into the eye of a castle ruin that watches us from the hill, and yet without you I am always *seule*.

Alone, under a cold moon, I wander cobblestones, home to my bed. There, I stare at the Van Gogh stars swirling outside my window. I pray when I sleep you will come to me and sing the song that was carved on my heart before I took this body.

Chante pour moi, mon amour divin, s'il te plaît.

My soul will rest best when God writes the chapter of our story wherein my marrow melts back into your bones.

Cave Painting: Magdalene's Mania

Today, I wrote your name on the walls again and again and again. Your syllables roared beneath ancient elk, carved into the stone by hands long since dust. In a flurry of drums, I conjured you.

If only the people could see me with these moths in my hair, my face dripping with dew. They wouldn't be able to handle it. They have sanitized sainthood. Always, they leave out the horror story parts, though the holy books have the good sense to keep them in.

What is truth?

My halo is made of moss.

The wind is ravenous, licking at the mouth of the cave. I wonder if it wants to eat me, swallow me down, slurp me up into the net of eternity strung from star to star, the moon lassoed and rearing, the frenzied sun surging, ready to erupt.

I sing until I see God, until I see you, which is the same thing for me. I have learned more about forever, about me, from your eyes than I have learned from all the holy books in the world.

I lie still on the stone floor for hours, staring at my hands, not believing what I am.

So what about us, my love? What about the light we are made of? What about our Big Secret?

You may not recognize me next time we meet. While I was sleeping, lilacs grew between my toes. A lone, heartsick sparrow built a nest in the nook of my shoulder blade. I feed him berries at low tide.

When I am high, you walk to me on every wave of blue that rolls in. I drown in you.

One day, while lying on a hilltop, stone cold sober, I heard a voice say, "Don't worry. You can breathe under water." I never talk about it. They lock people up for shit like that.

I believe in Divine Madness, because I have lived it.

A Call to Arms, Written in the Ruins of an Ancient Castle, Just Before the Rain

When I die do not count me among the so-called saints, the fearful ones who bit their tongues, sealed their eyes shut, stabbed their ears with withering fingers, bowed low before kings and priests born to make meat of men and women, sent to subdue the magic of earth, and by some sick alchemy change her heaven to hell. They weave an inferior magic, black threads spun of witch hunts, wars, the roars of tractors come to flatten forests, inquisitions, subdivisions, the screams of starving children.

Instead, count me among the mad ones who danced as if fires burned beneath their feet, who opened their eyes wide and saw everything, who swallowed the universe whole, who screamed truth from hilltops fringed with yellow weeds more precious than gold, who hold the laws of sacred magic in their bones, who found God in cyclones and monkeys and anemones, who slept little but sang much, who understood The Almighty was not scribbled in scrolls and carved in stones, but was written on the platelets of their blood, who loved not with their minds but with their marrow, who knew the straight and narrow road leads inward, not out, who shouted "no" to apathy, to tyranny, to lies.

Brothers, sisters of light, the night is almost over. Greet the dawn. Our backs buckle. We have labored long in the moonless black, but now is not the time to sleep, to die, to calcify into shells of the miracles we once were. Do not be pacified by their empty ease, their greed, their insatiable need for gold, gold, and more gold, pagan altars of cold, worthless stones built on the holy bones of our children.

Our "fuck no" cries must echo the whole world over, set the stratosphere ablaze, upend the graves of dead prophets, burn through the gray illusion that hovers heavy over the surface of the earth, give birth to the heaven that burns at the molten center of our mother's sacred core.

Scrying

And the waters moved, and there was you.

And the mirrors flashed, and there was you.

And the crystals danced, and there was you.

And the candles melted, and there was you.

And the tea leaves congealed, and there was you.

And the cards fell, and there was you.

And the flames leapt, and there was you.

And the visions loomed, and there was you.

And the seers intoned, and there was you.

And the dreams drifted, and there was you.

When I opened my eyes, the sunrise

drew a picture of you on the horizon,

and I finally knew everything inside

my heart looked like your face.

Pythagorean Prayer

I.

I have turned in on myself,

a blossom unflowering, bleeding brown

a beehive collapsing, seeping honey

a black hole swallowing space and time

until nothing remains but

this cold ache

this stony place where you once sat

the hole I refuse to fill

with anything but your missing face.

Dogs howl in the streets

as if crying can bend time backward

turn what is into what was.

I do not want that.

I want something that has never been

not in this world

not in this life.

II.

The knife of your spirit comes to me in the night

cuts me until I bleed visions.

I see your pores leaking light.

I save every sacred word you say.

When day breaks this time,

I beg you,

do not float away.

Do not evaporate like mist.

I have already been kissed by death.

I am alive only because I love a ghost

that may someday slip back into his body

and run to me.

III.

Allergic to sun, I moonbathe.

Trees buckle knobby knees,

bend to pet me.

I let them.

In lieu of men

I love star-beams.

I give my body to the wind.

The sky licks me.

I spread my legs wide,

let Life inside.

I am never

and always

alone.

IV.

I have given up on trying to understand.

Madness eschews method by definition.

It is only this:

Make it through today,

then sleep,

and his ghost will creep to your bedside.

Maybe this time

when midnight splits,

and a slit of horizon

gives birth to tattered tangerine sky,

he will un-die, come in the flesh

riding on the back of something mortal and meaty.

A lucky, buckle-backed horse, rescued from a glue factory.

A rusted out truck, lifted from the city dump.

He will shuck the corn of you,

swallow you whole

lend his lips to your skin.

Your sins will be undone.

You will bow before him.

You will call him God

because always, his invisible spirit has been

The alpha and omega

The unseen mover

The bread of life

The silent prayer

The only thing that has kept you breathing.

V.

Sun still seeps from aching ground.

You are all around me and nowhere at once.

I stumble on through a thick night

blighted by stuttering owls and thunder.

Red rocks rip my feet.

Yuccas tear me.

I stay silent, having become accustomed

to perpetual gutting.

Crickets speak in tongues.

Wind runs fingers through my hair,

whispering my name in your voice.

Come, come, come.

When you call, I can't run.

My shattered legs betray me.

Am I undone completely?

VI.

Unraveled, I clatter like lightning over rain swollen clouds.

Pointless, I splatter like a wandering squall, sloshing

and scattered upon boulders. What is left of me

when there is no you?

A pile of bones,

A puff of hair,

Three ounces of air,

A stiletto.

Have I given my best meat to the dogs?

VII.

If only grief were good for something.

If only I could weave it into a coat

wrap it around me

keep out the cold,

but grief is made of nothing but holes.

In dreams, I braid your hair into a cocoon

crawl in, sleep peacefully, finally.

VIII.

Starlight splints my shattered bones.

Soon I'll be ready to run.

Whisper again, my love.

Come, come, come.

I buy new legs

a bag of silk fresh from the worm

butterfly wings, still wet,

and a kite.

Cocoon cracks.

I poise on a branch, ready to take flight.

My tongue becomes a proboscis

penetrates the dark.

Night's nectar tastes like you.

IX.

When midnight cracked, the black rolled back.

You walked out from nothing, being light,

and there was my reason to breathe.

Newborn star, fall into my mouth.

Be a coin to this corpse.

Pay the ferryman to row me

to the place of the deathless.

Infinite love, breathe your life

into the mud of me.

X.

Through you I rise to God.

Polyxeni's Pentecost

We speak the same forgotten language,

up to our necks in dreams

sent by a Jesus only we can see. He wears

the clothes of a smalltime rock star, whispering

we can walk on water. We try, going under

frequently, drowning daily, giving each other

mouth to mouth, raising one another from the dead.

We take turns Lazarus-ing, try our hands

at rolling the stone away from the tomb.

Every time it rumbles, we cry,

"There it is! A miracle."

Every time, we are surprised.

When we speak of the rapture, we sing,

"We never saw it coming,

but of course, it came like this.

How could it have been any other way?"

When the holy ghost falls,

Polyxeni sniffs my hair, declares

I smell like sulfur and stars.

Rewinding Yoko Ono

Another whiskey Wednesday, and what do I write?

That I hate tequila because it killed you? That hearing the Hail Mary translated to fluent trailer trash was the worst thing that ever happened to me, a sick alchemy that made me want to off myself, but I on-ed myself instead? That your jealous, hellish lover Courtney-Loved you into a corner? That your mediocre mistress Yoko-Ono-ed you to death, and so what, because resurrection is a thing? That just last night, I saw you walking on water in your sleep, and I loved you for it? That together we went fishing for Christ fish, and neither of us came up empty? That I know now I was always the prophecy painting of the girl with the bomb hidden behind her back, and it's just about to blow me to kingdom come?

(Watch me fly.)

I am not sad, exactly, because I live in the lining of the veil between worlds, where always I can hear your voice, and those of seraphim, and demons, and gods. You taught me to surf water slides that arc through the center of the earth. There are crystals there, and kaleidoscopes. I ride waves with my mind. Always, I think, *Take me to him, take me to him,* and the dream does. I am addicted to your eyes. I have been schooled to swallow fire. I speak with the tongues of angels. I too walk on water, though it is always you who saves me when I drown. Everything is a sacrament to me. The leaves. The buckets of rain. The paper bags blowing in the wind. I worship waterfalls. I bow before Brahman rams. I sing the song of the Great-I-Am, written in the chirps of crickets.

Another whiskey Wednesday, and what do I write?

That I still love you (again)? That wolves dream prettier things that humans ever will? That I have followed the trail of truth to the core of everything, and it burns? That you live there? That your eyes are the color of suns? That yellow was never the right word to describe morning? That dawn breaks at the edge of a lake where herons call, and you crouch there always, fishing on the fringe of that water, dragging Jesus into your fists?

(Watch you fly.)

I am the queen who stooped to lick the hem of your garment. I am the hated whore the rabble stoned in the streets. I am the vein that runs along the edge of the leaf, the one the vicar insect walks on because it's narrow, and harrowing, and something else, something bugs don't know how to describe. And neither do I. The straight and constricted path grew out of your eyes, and I loved it, even when it snapped me in half.

I made a pilgrimage to your Mecca last night. You laughed as you danced through fire. You told me the laughing was the dancing. You told me if I do not smile, the flames will eat all of me alive. I smiled. I kissed you. I tasted your tongue. I married your insanity.

Another whiskey Wednesday, and I will write this:

We are both crazy, thank God. These people's sanity will be the death of them.

Let's un-pave parking lot and put up a paradise.

Le Pain

The streets all look the same after a while
Paris, Madrid, Florence, Prague, Brussels
differentiated only by lettering on signs.
I am in a cafe in London. The menu boasts *"le pain."*
Beside me, two old women chatter in French.
I eavesdrop the way I did in Nimes, understanding
something about a husband (or son?), the rain, a cake
as I look out the window watching for you
like always. Even when you're a continent away
I wait. The miracle of you happens
from time to time. Why not today,
way on the other side of the world?
People win lotteries, strike oil, find
bags of cash in floorboards.
Why not me? I remember a day,
decades ago, sitting in a window like this one.
Boise? Barcelona? Who knows?
But you came, and all the pain
I'd ever known washed clean
as you passed. I gasped. You didn't even see
me seeing you, but my veins coiled themselves
into the shape of your name. Your hair was longer
then. You wore brown leather, and if I had to paint

a picture of forever, I'd paint your eyes as you passed,

staring at the sidewalk's brick face being marred

a millimeter at a time by snow freckles. Today, I wait

again, remembering the way you looked at me

across the bar that night, your eyes saying everything

I ever wanted to hear. You showed up after all those years.

I'll never forget. And when I die, I imagine

what I will remember of this life is the big things:

The pain. The births. The deaths. The way my heart

sputtered and restarted when I watched out windows

in Edinburgh Rome Jerome Gnome Tombstone

and once in a while, thunder rolled, the sky split open, spitting

snow, and I won the lottery, struck gold,

because you came.

A Stab at Graffiti Salvation

I drove a million miles to find heaven today, newborn spring sizzling the skyline pink. I found God in a mural, white braids, brown hat. He didn't shine, but behind him, a silvery moon burned like it meant business.

I told him, "I'll be looking for love in all the wrong places, hanging out across the street, eating lemon cake, drinking coffee, if you want to meet. It's a shot in the dark, but what's a girl supposed to do?"

"Spring forward, fall back," he proclaimed. The words seemed to have a deeper meaning, cartwheeling from his tongue.

"I'm not dumb, but I don't get it," I whispered, wishing I spoke fluent God.

He smiled, or tried, but bits of bird wing and clotted paint kept him from moving his eyes. The grin didn't even touch his teeth.

I asked him if he liked my heart. He said it smelled like rain. A train trundled by, or a trolley. It was hard to tell in the dark. He handed me a wad of cash, said, "Wait for your miracle. I'm trying."

My heart banged against my ribs, a crazed rat in a cage. I wandered past a drunken beetle. It didn't want to talk. I left flowers on the sidewalk, seven shreds of butterfly wing, buckets of acid rain, three strands of graying hair, two bolts of rusty lightning, a wad of gently used gum, purple graffiti that says love's name, so close to God's toes, he'd kick it if he wasn't frozen on brick like that, his feet buried deep in asphalt.

God tried to smile. I rested my head on the tip of His oil paint thumb, waiting for him to come down.

Whitsun

This is not another heartbreak poem. I am not alone. I do not miss you. My life is not a waking death. I have never been anywhere without you.

In France, you laid your head in my lap in castle ruins. Flowers grew fast, mimicking one of those time lapse nature shows where seeds become full- fledged roses in 30 seconds flat. Vines wound themselves between your fingers, necklaced your throat, crowned you king of everything that ever mattered–guitars and love and orange blossoms and the pink pads on the bottoms of bobcat kittens' feet. I watched you sleep, wrote odes to your not-there knuckles, your missing kneecaps, your invisible eyelids.

When I died in New Orleans, beads dangled from trees. Decked out in bangles and bell bottoms, street psychics cackled as I screamed. The waning moon un-beamed, went black. Smokestacks buckled. You came and reached for me. "Stay!" I shrieked. The boiling ground sucked you away.

The day I looked down on London from the Eye, you told a joke, something about a baroque bar and a goat, and we laughed. Later, rain pelted us. Umbrella-less, we ducked under an awning until it drooped, ruptured, and drenched us. "Surrender to the baptism," you whispered, held my face, and kissed me hard. Red busses streaked, and we sneaked into an alley, just behind the cemetery where Mark Bolan lies. Our eyes gave birth to visions. The downpour washed us clean. Our guanine reconfigured, rewrote our DNA. The holy spirit fell that day. I sang the hymns of seraphim.

And you. You raised the dead.

Secret Identity

When the hostess at the swanky San Miguel rooftop bar said we needed to go back where we came from--we with our tanless skins and "pronouncing-the-H-in-*hola*" mouths--I felt less offended than surprised, and curious, wishing to do an autopsy of my heart in that moment. So this is what it feels like to be on the wrong end of racism, I thought.

As we descended the marble staircase, my friends spewed outrage, but I remained calm, remembering all those times white women crossed the street to avoid having to share a sidewalk with my brown father. Now, my brother, who stole all of our daddy's melanin, worries that his girlfriend's daddy won't like him because he's Mexican. I watched an old man hobble by, wondering if he looked the way my father might, had he lived, feeling an inexplicable thrill at finally being treated the way I always would have if my skin hadn't been lying for me all along.

Once I was in a Lorca play. Someone in the audience shouted, "Preach it, gringa," during my monologue. I wanted to stop the show, let him know I am not a gringa, at least not all the way. My grandmother Carmen Sanchez spoke fluent Spanish and piled my plate high with green chile and sopapillas.

If only my brother had been there at that rooftop bar. Then we would have gotten our jicama tacos and pomegranate margaritas. Then he would have been the rich brown man with many *stupida* gringas dangling from his arm. He never would have had to mention that one of those dumb white women was his sister. He could have passed a whole evening saying *cerveza*, not beer, watching a waxing moon melt over the jagged chapel in the distance. For one night, my pale blue eyes, my skin that burns when it gets too close to a lightbulb, might have made my life harder than his.

The next bar was on the ground, but they gave us smiles and margaritas (no pomegranate) in exchange for our American dollars. I drank it slowly, relishing the tang, thinking at long last, I was my father's daughter.

Quand Devrait-Elle Voler ?

We all want wings. I'll buy mine, sinewy, made of steel, lifting me high until men scuttle below, bees on fruit sucking up juice, spinning honeyed magic.

I'll become a bee myself, settle on the Big Apple's skin, sleep curled in a cocoon of Times Square dreams and spotlight beams. I'll skitter along the seam that lies between the Atlantic and the land, find the hand of the man who was born to die to live again. I'll take his fingers on my tongue.

Tarry sands have damned my ocean of gold. This river runs thin. Twenty-two angels have turned their coats, leaving me with just three pennies and a note my father wrote me: "Stay strong until the end, and when The Man calls, you'll know it's time to soar."

So I wait for the phone to ring. Winds roar, threatening the walls. Day-of-directions are no good. I must be given the time to rise. I'll do anything to find God. I'll scale the Empire State Building, but tickets to heaven are twice the price when you don't buy them in advance. I don't have cash to chance it.

My eyes burn with a billion calendar suns. Moon phases phase me. I want numbers, man, the day the hand will slide into my mouth. Monday? Tuesday? Wednesday? God, rig the game in my favor, you dig? Dot my dreams with specificity. If you can't speak yourself, send a saint. Peter knows his shit. He was always the rock, and I knew it. (Who knew The Son's #1 wore flannel?)

Say: "The queen wants a fortune teller, a crystal ball, a string of tarot cards. The whys have been scribbled in the space behind her eyes for centuries. She has the where. She wants some whens.

We all want wings. I'll buy mine, gossamer webs of spring. I'll lick electric liberty's torch, drain all that's left in her dwindling stream for one last chance to drink from the hand of God.

Part 3:

Big Bang

No one knew it was Easter then.

No one sang of resurrection.

They only hunched on stone stoops with sullen eyes,

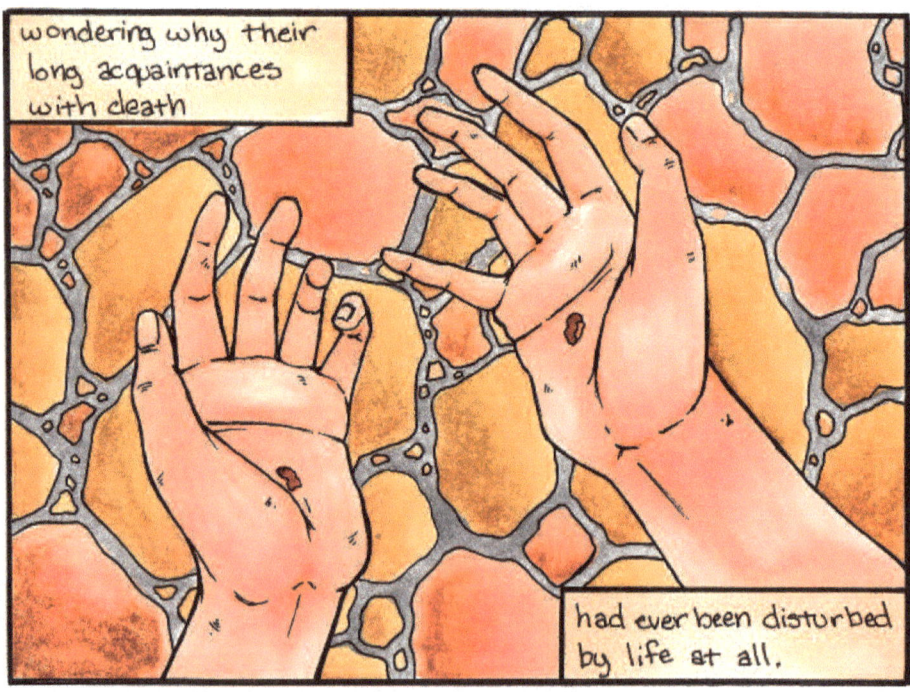

wondering why their long acquaintances with death

had ever been disturbed by life at all.

Who wakes on this miracle morning seething, percolating rage,

as the coffee maker steams,

not knowing that today might be the day that changes everything?

Kitsched

You have bedazzled the stonewashed jean jacket of my skin,
studded my flesh with glitter, sequins, and stars. You have
expanded my mind like a *Chia* pet, synapses sprouting stems
and leaves, making unicorned shrubs of my dreams.
You have dipped the *Sea Monkey* of my heart in cool water.
Its styrofoam grows, bending my ribs 'til they crack.
Your *Ginsu* knives have sliced through the gristly meat
of my soul like it was melted butter. (And they're still sharp!)
You have turned my muted voice into a *Mr. Microphone.*
"Hey good lookin', I'll catch you later," I intone all night long.
I have become a Lionel Richie song. If I'm not careful, my
freckles will reconfigure, forming a constellation mirroring a
White Snake cassette cover, the one
with the heavy metal viper hatching from an egg.
Strangers will point out my resemblance
to David Hasslehoff. My bugle-ish boy, from the moment
I skidded to a stop on that desert highway, determined
to ascertain the brand of your jeans, I knew when you touched
me, I would sprout some bling. Thanks
to you, a tiny *Rubix Cube* provocatively
dangles from each of my glistening teeth.

Satori

I fell in love with a squirrel one day when he skittered across my path. At first, it was a passing crush. I thought, "What a cute squirrel." But then I noticed--really saw--the intricate white hairs fringing the brown fluff of his tail, and I was utterly besotted, overcome by the pretty of him.

I saw the red leaves fallen beneath his feet, and I thought, "Lucky leaves, getting to touch the miracle of those tiny toes." And then I noticed the exquisite network of veins running through the leaves, and I thought, "Lucky squirrel, getting to touch the magic of those leaves." I fell in love with them too, and the whole world exploded into a web of wonder. For ten perfect seconds, I forgot who I was.

That was the day I found out what purple smells like, and that spinach tastes like what cows must long for when they dream of grass. I learned that the separation between trees and sky is invisible, and that bugs who walk on water do know they are replicating Jesus, but they try not to get too cocky about it. I discovered that the world is chocked full of red, and if you smile at people fast, before they have time to think, they drop their masks for a moment and smile back. I noticed that my own mask is torn. I realized there are peek holes in everything, passages to another world. Everything is a wardrobe leading to Narnia. Everything is a train headed to Hogwarts.

Only no one looks because after all, we have bills that must be paid.

Taken?

I could say my heart belongs to someone else,

but that would be a half truth, at best. A quarter truth.

A tenth truth. Here is the whole shebang: Both hemispheres

of my brain also belong to him, as well as my torso,

my toenails, and the prickly bumps on my kneecaps.

My hair follicles are in love. If you study my fingerprints

under a blue light supplied by a medium who specializes

in languages spoken mostly by dead men, you will see

that the whorls spell my beloved's name in ten forgotten

alphabets. When I went to the dentist, he asked me

if I had noticed my teeth were buzzing, and if I had,

did I realize they were humming my beloved's favorite song?

My doctor worried when she saw that my entrails

had twisted themselves into a reasonable facsimile

of the date of his birth. Twice, my waxer has asked me

to please stop tweezing my eyebrows to replicate his smile.

But I'm not. They just grow that way. Every cell in my body

bends in his direction. If I were a map, I'd be a boring one.

Of course, every road would end with him. You've heard that

one before. And yes, every river would sprint

into his ocean. He would be the guru crouched

on the snowy peak of every single mountain.

The moose in the forests would constantly bellow his name.

At the heart of each pyramid, you would find a mummy,

and when you opened its coffin, a pharaoh him would sit up.

A thousand bucks says you'd love him too, on sight.

Do you get me? I'm a hopeless case, a goner. Do not

resuscitate. It's done. I'm his. There is no going back,

not when the bumps of my spine mimic his laugh in braille.

When my confessor asked me why, I said: "He drives

the darkness from my bones. He makes me walk on water."

High Calling

When God called, I answered,

though I didn't hear her ringing at first.

It sounded like sand in my ears, or pavement,

stone streets gone rogue

wetting my dreams with concrete.

But I answered the next day

gave her my back

said, "Strap those wings on tight.

I'm ready to fly.

Eve's fruit was underrated.

Feed that apple to me twice."

God obliged, said "Your flight to Eden is booked.

Show up a day late, in style."

Tonight, the moon hangs heavy

a weight around my waist

dragging me down

through the slick slog of modern mundanity

but when the sun comes up

tomorrow, I'll soar.

By the time the moon opens

her one white eye again

I'll be in another world

licking electric lips

dancing with the light.

The night is heavy.

God, wait for me.

I'll probably be drunk

and unprepared for an encounter

of this magnitude. If it pleases you,

adopt an attitude of compassion.

Laissez-faire seems fair.

I haven't pedicured my toes in months.

The soles of my shoes are shot.

I threw the dice twice, bought a ticket

to your promised land.

Take my hand.

I'll be waiting.

Like the fabled City of God,

I'll be awake from dawn to dawn.

I'll host an eternity of ragers.

I'll never sleep again.

The Lens

Love you. Not just the pretty parts of you. The wide eyes and the killer smile. Not just the part of you that has good politics and sound theology, the part of you that loves the right person perfectly with a gift of $50 roses and an exquisite box of chocolates. But the parts of you that are ugly. The pimples and the cellulite. The part of you that secretly answers the big questions with a quavering, "I don't know." The part of you that forgets her mother's birthday. The part of you that drank a box of wine alone last night, weeping because nobody loved it. The part of you that ate the whole bowl of cookie dough. The part of you that can't get her shit together. The part of you that loves the wrong people in all the wrong ways. Love that person.

This is the hard part, loving this person. Because it's easy to love the perfect person, or it should be, but it's not, because you know that no matter how flawless your mask, it's not really you. You are the one that falls in love with the bad ones. You are the one that sings off key and keeps whiskey bottles under her bed unopened, just in case. You are the one that runs from the sun because you don't want people to see what you look like in the light. You are all kinds of fucked up. And yet, you must love you. All of you. This is the part of being human that will make or break you. It's not about how much of you you can get right. It's about how much of you you can love, even when you get it all wrong.

Right now, right where you are standing, if you could pull the camera away from the close up, pull the lens all the way into forever, and see the intricate, tragic, glorious beauty that is you, you would love you.

I know what you're thinking. If I love those parts of me, I will fuck up. Of course you will. You will fuck up epically. You were born to fuck up. If life were meant to be lived perfectly, it would come with a rule book, a rule book that is not open to interpretation, a rule book that makes sense. It doesn't. By virtue of the very nature of life, no matter what choices you make today, one night, you will lie screaming in your bed, hating yourself, because of the choices you make. Love you anyway.

I know what you are thinking. What if I get it wrong? You will get it wrong. You have no chance of getting it right. Did you really think the point of life was getting it right? Did you really think your little brain could wrap itself around the vastness of all that is and get the perfect answer? You will answer wrong, and wronger, and wrongest. Love you anyway.

I know what you are thinking. What if people hate me? Of course they will hate you. Did you think there was some way to live quietly, kindly, flawlessly enough that another fucked up human, a human who is unable to love herself, would not look at you and see something in you that reflects her own pain and hate you for it? Did you really think that you could live in a world of fucked up humans and somehow come out unscathed? Live true, and love you, and let the people who hate you hate you. If you lived a lie, people would still hate you. It would just be different people. At least the people who hate you when you live true hate you honestly. At least they hate the real you. All kinds of people will hate you. Beautiful people will hate you. Ugly people will hate you. Smart people will hate you. Dumb people will hate you. Love you anyway.

You will fuck up. You will get it wrong. People will hate you. And in spite of all this, in spite of all the failure and wrongness, in spite of all this two in the morning screaming, this whiskey drinking, this loving bad people in bad ways, this not getting your ass off the couch and getting to the gym, this mess that you are, love is the only lens that will allow you peace, will let you look down on you, curled up on the couch, watching pointless television, feeling hopeless, love is the thing that will look down on all the inexplicable unknowable unanswerable vastness that is you and see you for what you are.

A walking miracle.

Parisian Kintsugi

The bus trundled, and out the window
centuries old stone tenements loomed
made modern with spray paint scrawls
their iron balconies spruced up by *les femmes*
wearing red and blue, hanging laundry
as women had for hundreds of years. And over there
the Eiffel Tower lived up to its name, towering,
as it always had, as long as you could remember
and then back into times you couldn't.

A knife slitting the Parisian sky, making it bleed
sleet. A needle stabbing your American eyes,
forcing you to remember your last glimpse.

Years before, driving at night, beleaguered, scared,
short on gas. Then, the Eiffel Tower glowed
in the distance, a beacon not a weapon.
Now, the bus lurched on, the Eiffel Tower gone, disappeared
in the rearview, but still there
because you knew that today's glimpse was one
of thousands, that in fact, there was no time,
just snapshots, various expressions of the same scenes,
the same truths, the same people

again and again and again
static monuments and moments
shot from different angles through eternity

The way you knew when you first held your baby boy

that someday he would tower over you, pick you up

and spin you around as if you were weightless

when you stepped off a plane from France. The way

you understood when your toddler daughter teetered

toward you having caught you horrifyingly naked

with a bastard who didn't love you and pressed

your clothes into your hands, her bearing regal,

her eyes wise, as if she already knew the ways

in which the wrong men could cheapen you,

had already diminished you. "Remember,

you are a queen," she seemed to say,

and you wondered if she had once been

your mother, if you took turns playing protector.

In France, they called you La Reine, echoing her sentiment.

The way you accepted the first time

you glimpsed The One's forever eyes

that he would be the love of your life

that he was the love of all of your lives
and dressed as love, he would do what love does best
break you and make you again, something stronger.

The truest unraveled and rewoven
tapestry you could be. The way
bones knit themselves together
again after snapping. The way
skin grows back thicker after bleeding.

He would shatter you and regather the shards,
reimagining your soul as a vase
whose cracks are grouted with treasure.

The way the Japanese say
that broken things are more valuable
because of the gold that shimmers
in their mended moments.

You saw time as a spiral, a frozen, static thing,
a series of points on a map. When you draw
the camera back, out into forever time is nothing
more than Einstein's stubbornly persistent illusion.

Reality is an eternal, unchanging snapshot

and death is nothing more

than the blinking of a shutter

and love is love is love

and towers are towers are towers

and everything about this ride we are on

adds up to heaven

and all there is

is life.

Not I Do, But I Am

You set the desert sand on fire. Choirs sing in your hair.
I took a spaceship through time, and there you were, pulsing,
the beginning of my everything. I rode a submarine to the
center of my bones, and there you were,
swimming in my marrow. When I write you, I feel
the missing words, the ones humans haven't invented yet
shimmering in the spaces between sounds. The best poem
I ever penned about you was silent. It prismed the sky around
it, making tiny rainbows in raindrops. They ask me why. Why
this? Why that? Why won't you come here? Why did you
go? The answer is always you. The answer is always because
they are not you. When mountain night
is rocked and rattled by ancient wind, I sleep
in your invisible arms. I feel you spinning in my platelets.
The answer is always, I love you. The question is always,
Where are you? (I need to be there.) The answer
is because I could never be in love with them.
I am made of in-love with you. My love is atomic.
It's TNT times ten billion. It explodes my skin
and seeps into the air around me, making me radioactive.
They ask me, Why are you on fire? I say,
Because there is a him, and he makes an inferno
of my dreams. Smoke rises from my hair, a burnt offering.

It's not that I choose you. It's that if there was no you
there would be no me. It's not that I marry you.
It's that I am marriage to you. It's that you sing in my soul
deep in the echoes of the mini-big-bang that volcanoed
me into being. Before that eruption, there was you.
The stories got it wrong. I wasn't a rib. I was a bump sleeping
on the tip of your tongue until you spoke
and made me live, saying, If I made a queen,
how would she be? And when you said, She
would be like this, I jumped from your mouth
grew a thousand miles and cannonballed into the river
that flowed from your ribcage. There and then,
you baptized me. Tonight, there is no moon
only flurries of snow mothing in cold porchlight
growing wings, whipping windows white. My body
tangles, limbs twisted to form the first letter
of your name. Tonight, your heartbeat thrums
in the sizzling cymbals of my kneecaps.
My soul's first-last-and-only husband,
my very quarks sing your praise.

Meeting the Nameless Mother

Awake, oh sleeper. A song lives in those hills, past the purple flowers that grew from the seeds The Mother left in her footprints when she passed. Lick the dawn. Swallow the sunrise whole. Let the branches grow, wrapping themselves around your legs, making them strong and thick. Become the goddess you were born to be. Let the river drown out the voices of the demons who whispered their lies in the night, who stole your eyes so you could no longer see yougodyougodyougod.

You. God.

Demons are made of dust. They disperse in the breeze. You fall to your knees and whisper. Nothing. The name of God is only *hhhhhhuuuhhh*. It is only breath. It cannot be said. Say it, and you take away the sacred. Make it a thing of this earth. Or say it, but do not think when you do that God will stay within the box you have made. Let her dance outside those walls you erected from so much breath. Let her sing, "Death is an illusion, and stars from far away galaxies pulse the truth of the ages, which is all there is is *hhhhhhuuuhhh*. You are *hhhhhhuuuhhh*, You are born from stardust. Breathe."

Breathe God in like oxygen. Hold the stone of her on your tongue. Taste the salt of her sweat. Let her seep into your pores. Make her close. Make her you. Even in the darkest nights, when you were sleeping in hell with those demons, she has always been, will always be, yours.

.

Capiche?

I miss you the way I'd miss my toenails if they were pulled out by the mafia, or the way I'd miss my eyes if I stared into the sun until I went blind. I miss you the way a madman misses his mind, achingly, in starts and fits, almost forgetting I ever had you sometimes. I miss you the way Jesus missed his skin when they flailed it from his back. Call it blasphemy, but I won't lie. I cry, "My God, my God, why have you forsaken me," on the daily, but what I mean by God is you, even though you're not gone, just locked up in that matchbox with a newborn swan, a few hairpins, and a bag of rocks.

Whales un-blue themselves, flinging their great, heaving bodies on the beach, tails thrashing, reaching for your wonder. Pirate ships give up their plunder, renounce their lives of crime, go straight. Tectonic plates shift when you sneeze. When you pass, lampposts bend, hissing yellow breath into smog tainted breeze, to ask if you're shamanic.

You drift to me like incense through the air conditioning vents of every rented room I find. You say my name in braille sometimes. You teach me to see in tongues. Once, I ran my hands over the rungs of the ladder of your rib cage, and I climbed a thousand miles. Your smile has become my anchor to this world. If not for you, I'd melt away, and I wouldn't care. A reverse Rapunzel, I'd follow the rope of my hair down, down, down, to the ground, then under.

Just now, mist you hovers over that chair in the corner, invisibly missing me, whispering the secrets of God in the rasping language of rattlesnakes maraca-ing through the window. Reptiles always shake after the rain, the way trains always blow their whistles when Nina Simone plays.

Last night, as stars cast pulsing purple over low-hanging clouds, I plucked a dream from your head, saw me in a subway. You were there. You smiled, and shards of moonlight hung from your hair, slicing your skin 'til it glowed. You took my hand and towed me to the other end of the world. I can't dance, but I followed you, and it worked out fine. My spine tingled when you touched my back, turning me. You had feet enough for two. I wanted to tell you I loved you, but you already knew, and anyway, you didn't have time for small talk.

You laid me on the rock of Gibraltar, made an altar of my lips. I laughed, took the miracle of you on my tongue, swallowed you whole the way a starving woman downs cool milk. The nighttime licked me alive, silk on my skin. You sang in the sinless language of Christ, and thrice, the train running past wept, so I knew Johnny Cash's ghost was on board. Roosters crowed in reverse, so I knew St. Peter had un-denied. I tasted your salt, so I knew I'd died and gone to heaven.

"Capiche?" you asked.

"Capito," I whispered.

Prufrock measured his life in coffee spoons. I measure mine in the bumps on your tongue.

What Magdalene Wrote in the Sand When the Mob Was Gone

Drop your rocks, boys. The Man picked me.

See, I lick Ganesh's trunk, kiss Guadalupe's Virgin

on her ever-shining cheek. At midnight, we three,

trinity, waltz on the silvery waters of distant planets.

Light seeps from the slender moons rising at the tips

of my toes. I dance through meadows unseen by men.

They think my face is pretty? They should see my soul.

If they only knew the secrets that my platelets keep.

After three days, I rose from my grave carrying magic

in my bones. I ate 777 pomegranates from Olympus's lushest

grove. This just in: my soul has been un-sinned.

The never-ending spiral of my belly button is a water slide

winding straight to the ice blue pool at the center

of the Eye of Horus. Insert chorus here, cue an angel choir.

Fall, sacred fire, fall. When they said the goddess

was a honey bee, I dove straight into the hive.

Ten thousand drones stung me alive, made my marrow

simmer. Secrets shimmer in my eyes. My DNA knows

everything there ever was to know. The tree of life grows from

my sternum. My chromosomes speak of God

in ancient languages understood only by ghosts

and swordfish. Exult, heavenly hosts! I have rewound

Judas's kiss, dismissed demons, leveled the gates of Sheol.

I un-shell mysteries like peanuts, swallow them whole.

My holy dreams stink like the bellies of oysters

giving birth to pearls. My visions flutter like rainbows

in oil puddles. My soul dangles, un-muddled, at the edges

of my earlobes. I have married the Christ. I wear

his silver ring on my toe. I have been un-slaved, un-stoned,

shamed in reverse. I know only one Master. He calls

me baby. For Him alone I bow. Who's a whore now, bitches?

I won't be raped again. My sacred cows

have been de-slaughtered. I have emerged from death

a daughter of light. My stilettos reek of interstellar travel.

Behold, I have unraveled and raveled again.

Lo, I glow I glow I glow.

Ohm

All of the love I ever wrote was just a way of saying his name a little longer. And saying his name was just another way of saying his eyes. And saying his eyes was just a long way of saying _____, that silent breath that God breathed when She exhaled the universe into existence, thinking it was very good. Did God dance that day? Did She sway to the sound of the spinning stars, wearing moons in her hair and Saturn's rings on the tips of her toes? Did She expose her breasts to The Sun and dare him to burn her? I think She must have been, must be, something like us when we are at our best, that moment of brilliant, brave tipsy that comes just before drunk, right before we fall off the precipice into the abyss, slurring come-ons to boys we never remember in the morning.

I think She must have been like him, the way that dent in his throat always made everyone who ever saw it dream of licking it long after he was gone. The songs he sang were a way of saying her name, and mine, drawing them out in forever chords and shuddering chants, and when he brought his lips to the harmonica, we felt what it meant to sleep neck deep in_____.

I have not always loved love. Some days I have cursed him, slept shaking with his invisible name tarnishing the red of my lips, cracking and turning them brown. His cruelty has shattered me, made me a glassless, bent window pane after the suicide bomber, left me standing in Hiroshima under death's glowing mushroom cloud, gasping for breath, and even that sound was _____.

Because it all meant the same thing. It meant that the day I first saw him sway under an exploding canopy of stars was the day I first met God, was the day I first understood my own name had nothing to do with vowels but was a song She sang that day when She first gave herself to The Sun, settled beneath his heat, opened herself wide, and cried, "Burn me, break me, incinerate me, make me the embers that glow at the center of these bones, leave me shuddering and alone, clawing at my face, wailing for the home of you, calling _____."

Radha's Death Bed

My Krishna, I loved you when our skin was blue,

and we danced among the flowers

while your flute sang my name

the one written on my bones, known only to you and God.

I loved you the way silence loved the Big Bang

the way darkness loved the Let There Be

the way the ocean loved the lands

as they tore forth from her womb.

Death is generosity, the way a seed

cannot really live until it splits.

My Krishna, until I was a flower that opened to you,

I never knew true sex is death and birth at once,

the abolition of self so a starry sky can take her place.

The one you adore, the one that makes you want to live,

the one that you would die for, becomes the ache that kills

you, that melts you down to nothing until you are not alive

or dead, but something other. Something blue.

A streaking comet. A crashing ocean. A god.

My Krishna, you are the only thing I ever wanted to write

and I cannot, you who has 10,000 faces hiding

beneath his skin, who won't stay the same for one moment,

long enough for me to catch my breath, to grasp

for even a split second the breadth of your beauty.

You hijack my body, my mind, my soul,

and then the sky. You turn the whole world blue.

My Krishna, I drown in you daily, and it is exquisite,

and fearsome. I die every night in your arms, gasping for air.

But I return again and again and again and again and again

because once you have seen the face of God, you kiss it

though you know proximity to the fire of creation

will burn you down to bones and build you new again.

My Krishna, every night for a thousand years I will die

with your body inside mine. Every morning

until forever, I will rise to love you again.

The Book of Him

The boy at the bar asks, "What book is that?" and I want to say:

It is the book of him, it is always the book of him, everything is the book of him. He is the cracked vodka bottle and the mangy cat and the homeless man with blighted red skin who needs the voices to SHUT THE FUCK UP. He is the salt on these nuts and the gray at the waiter's temple. He is this wine as it turns my mouth the taste of the Spanish countryside. He is the blister on my heel. I read him when I chose this red dress, when I painted my lips, when I outlined my eyes like Cleopatra. I took a photo of that mural because the hand reminded me of his. He is the shred of lettuce wilting its way back to dust on the floor and the brown spot left on the ceiling when it snows. He is the neon sign spilling green into the walkway, the pedestrians slipping in its gunk. He is the peonies that wanted rain and died of thirst. If I lifted the stone at the corner of this building, I would find his name carved there, his birthdate, the secret of his never-death. I would know finally that this life was just a big *Where's Waldo* game written by him, only everything is Waldo. Waldo never hides. He is the only book I have ever read, kid, and if I read you, you will be him minus something, and I will hate you for it. Don't waste your money on me, Jeff, Sven,

Pedro, William, Serge, Bo, Lamar, Brian, Santos, Lee you are all him, and less than him, and I promise you've never read my book.

From Magdalene to the Risen Christ, A Prelude to Ascension

My love, today I heard
your tombstone crack.
The sound of your resurrection
shook the pillars of the sky.
Stars shook loose like gemstones
from the velvet cloak of night.
Volcanoes erupted.
Death trembled and died.
You have been uncrucified.
And now my king,
like me, you rise.
I have gone to prepare a place for you.
Come to me there, that paradise
of winding stairs, cobbled streets, and holy waterfalls.
Over the wind tossed river
a stone bridge arcs like a hissing cat.
A fat woman plays her violin.
Sins rise from skin to evaporate
like mist into the cool womb of Mary's night.
I will stand watch there, my starving stare
half dead for want of your face, whispering your name
Isa, my own Isa, bone of my bones, flesh of my flesh.

The shame of our deaths forgotten,

I'll wait until your light blots ink horizon

spattering dark with dawn.

Homecoming

I wandered the world searching

only to find my heart

was always buried in this desert

where I was born.

I didn't need champagne. I needed dirt.

I didn't need mansions. I needed trees.

I didn't need money. I needed the moon.

I didn't need parties. I needed prickly pear fruit

purple, tart, infesting my tongue with barbs,

and even the impaling feels like heaven.

I didn't need a million lovers. I needed one perfect soul.

Yours. It comes to me now, gliding over stones

like the tongue of the wind. It licks me

from top to toenails. I bask in the glory

of your spirit saliva, laughing at how crazy

it sounds when I write it down like that.

How did I imagine space and time could ever steal our love?

What was I drinking anyway, pretending to be like them?

Why would a wild woman like me ever want

this world's safe version of sane?

What did I mean when I said I was poor?

Didn't I know my bones were encrusted with pearls of truth?

Didn't I see every jewel in the sky was mine?

My fingers dig in, marrying the soil.

I baptize me in desert stones.

Dear world, a confession: I have always been

my father's daughter. I have always seen visions.

I have always dreamed dreams. I have always

heard the voices of angels in the breeze.

 Dear world, a revelation: It is always Christmas

if you take the time to notice. The pines dangle

with cones full of pinon nuts, red birds, moonlight tinsel.

The wind sings of the birth of redemption.

The mountains glitter with strings of stars.

Magdalene's Map

I have ascended

    come to the place

        where every molecule is infused with light

            I can see   the future

    and the past

        and the present

          as one.

Krishna's blue shines here.

    There is no fear.

        on the mountain of perfect love.

I scaled the gates of hell   to find my soul's true home

        tangled with screaming demons

wrestled with death itself   while ahead of me

    a Christ that looked nothing

        like the religious brochures

        walked, whispering,

Follow me home.   *Follow me home.*

As I climbed

    I lost everyone and everything

I thought I knew and owned

    because everyone and everything

I thought I knew and owned

    were links in the chains

binding me to hell's gates

I cannot show the way.   *I can only point to the door.*

      Look into your heart.

         Open it.

            Walk inside.

               Meet your Buddha

                  and your demons.

Your pride

      Your envy

         Your horror

          Your pain

            Dispatch them one at a time.

Climb

      Climb

        Climb

The road to heaven is not just narrow.

      It is steep and strewn about with terror and grief.

The road to heaven passes through hell

      because to get to paradise

      you must conquer the hell within your bones.

To find your true self

      you must kill the false self.

To live

      you must die.

         I do not fear death.

I have died.

I do not fear this life.

It is an illusion.

Perfect peace is true reality.

Forever

Unending

Miracles

Unmitigated

Light

Pure Love

Today, my hatred   melted

in the blaze of breaking dawn.

I pity those who stole from me along the way

strapped links from my chains around their necks   strutted

in their newborn diamond studded collars

while around them

the specter of death closed in

for them reality

because they believed it

as I once had.

Your mind is your prison.

To escape it

you must break it.

I cannot show you the path

only the door.

Look into your heart.

Find the ascended one

whose voice is a whispered

There must be something more.

Follow her

one agonizing beautiful step at a time

Your soul knows the way home.

It is harder than anything

you have ever imagined

and worth it.

Lose everything

to find your heaven.

The Christ said,

Many are called

But few are chosen

I say,

Many are called

But few choose

Because the way is horror.

It is not a formula for manifesting

a trip to Tahiti   a mansion   a romance.

It is not   a religion   a

free ticket to the sweet by and by.

It is a wretched road

to salvation

in the here and now that will cost

you everything.

It is a path

through your own insanity

into divinity.

It is a lifetimes long trip to heaven

via the hell the that lives in your

head.

Most see the door and say,

The price is too high.

Better to decorate my hellscape

and call it home.

A house here.   A new car there.

Another bout with bondage masquerading as love.

How about a fancy job?   How about a soothing church?

How about a seat in the cool kid's club?

Hell drives a hard bargain.

If you can be bought at any price, you will be.

Those I have lost along the way,

I want you to come with me.

Hear my voice now.   Open the door.

Climb

Climb

Climb

Beloved brothers and sisters   I cannot fuck you   or give

you the fleeting solace

you think you want from me.

To do so would be to

        descend again into hell.

            I can never go back,

but I can give you this

        My map to the door.

            The Christ in you.

                I love you.

                Come home.

Phenomenon

What is it to be a phenomenon
a force of nature, a slick bolt of lightning, gashing
burning orange the papery blue of the sky?
To ride waves of one's mind so thick
they drown out all other noises
the cacophony of tired voices
singing acquiescence into the wind,
their footsteps plodding slowly deliberately quietly
to the grave, unseeing unengaged
lest they upend stones, bend grass blades
cause cardinals to volcano from trees
explode into blurred red wing visions
and terrified thumb-throated song.

Oh, great mountain, blinding sea, trinity of life,
invisible edges of three white faces
that paint purple the walls of my horizon

let me not be that.

Rather, let me be a cat
that lolls and springs and tears
rats from their places

caring not for the screams of the landlord.

Let me be a frayed wire, electric hectic.

Let me shock to life those who dare touch me.

Let me never be a possession, a thin, reedy, well-kept thing.

Let me not be pretty, but thick-thighed and fierce.

Let me howl my name to the sky in the violet crease left

between the folded pages of midnight and dawn.

Let me stalk the backbone of God

searching for the nape of her neck.

When I find it, I will kiss it gently

leaving lipstick on her spine

making her mine,

calling her not God, but Mother.

She will smile, though she could tear me to pieces,

retract her claws and lick my lips.

She sees her heart in my eyes.

Night Vision

There are no words, just a shredding sound
and lightning sizzling the night until it blisters white
only the shimmering, rippling of sky that comes
when red flowers bloom out of nowhere in the desert
when creaking, twisted pines speak in the voice of heaven.
I have left this world for now. It has never been my home.
From far away, I watch me riding waves of moments
that have already drowned me in my dreams. Thank God
I know how this one ends. The future is written
on my eyelids. When I close them, I see tomorrow
and tomorrow and tomorrow. The hardest part of my life
is pretending to be surprised. In visions, you stand
just feet away, shining, calling me forward. I run to you,
and you move and move. I run and run, climbing
an invisible staircase until I hover over the world
far above everything I thought I knew. Last night, I laid myself
on a moss licked stone, an altar, and offered
myself to the gods of my father's mountain. They opened
their hands and rocked me. The stars blurred. A ghost moon
flickered, bearing witness. In their embrace, I married you
again. A sudden wind clattered in and blew out
the candle I had lit for you, momentarily, just long enough

to let me know I was in the throes of a miracle.

Your flame leapt back to life, casting shadows on the trees

that grew from the places my father's feet walked.

Machine gun dreams have never been able to part us,

not for one second. The spacetime continuum unravels

bowing low in the face of love. You are with me on the altar.

We lie together, naming stars kissing constellations,

swallowing eternity whole. Your invisible hand clasps mine.

Death flickers in the distance.

We are not afraid.

Inanna's Imperatives

To dream the color of the sun seeping
up through sidewalk cracks, the black,
buckled earth giving birth to light.

To let your skin be painted 12 shades
of red, long slick bloody strands.

To watch your hands weave slender stalks
of wheat into welcome mats for gods.

Allow the angels to enter, never mind
their disheveled hair. Catch rain in Styrofoam cups
and drink it. Say a prayer for the helpless things
the water bugs, the tadpoles, the naked baby birds,
yourself.

Remember that part in your hair was carved there
by God's razor blade just this morning.
Know you are never too old to live.
Know you are never too young to die.

Beautiful Little Things

Today I saw the way cream curled into my coffee, ribboning white between becoming a sunrise or an elephant's trunk. I saw a vase sprouting drug store carnations, sparkling in the sunlight, saying things about rainbows and chaos theory and the way fallen flowers beneath the snow promise to rise again, ricochet their way to resurrection. I touched a sparrow's skeleton, his skull sprouting mushrooms, whispering rumors of tomorrow's soup. I called him Advent and buried him beneath a shuddering shroud of yesterday's news. I heard the song of a cricket and thought maybe he was the reincarnation of John Lennon or Leonard Cohen. His hallelujahs filled the night like a choir, while in its place in the potbellied stove, the fire roared acquiescence to the wonders of the world. Not the seven but the seven trillion. And I remembered the way I'd seen a moth wing under a microscope that summer in Mary's County, Maryland, and how I, high as balls, said something about forever and fractions and fractals, while below my hungry eye, a once dead thing spiraled its blue way to infinity.

The Second Coming of Isis

This time, I will be prettier. I will ascend wearing diamonds in
my hair, having cobbled rainbowed wings together from drum
beats, guitar licks, the voices of gods trapped
in rock-n-roll songs, wrapped warm and jagged in the ragged
throats of women. This time, I will have new ears.
I will be deaf to taunts and reprimands of men, alive
to anthems of angels. This time, my fresh born eyes
will be blind to illusion, unconfused, undefiled, lifted
to the profusion of winged things that flit
through the membrane of space-time, those luminescent
specks of heaven strained out and erased by the stuttering
forebrains of mortals. My someday-sight will be 20/20
and lead me along a path invisible to the miracle-blind.
I will tread stepping stones rooted in the rock of Elysium.
This time, I will not walk alone. The sea that swallowed
my armies will vomit them onto land. The hand
of my mother will wipe Egypt clean of your graceless, greedy
faces. This time, I will wear chain mail. You will not see
my armor, but I will sport it in all its transparent glory.
The barbs demons sling at me will ricochet
and sink back into their own charred, scarred flesh.
This time, charlatans, rapists, murderers, witch hunters,
inquisitors, solicitors of humanity's basest instincts,

I will see you for what you really are. I will be untricked.
Uncursed. Unjinxed. Unseduced. I will slide aces
from my sleeve, and your flaccid deuces will slip impotently to
the floor. The shinery of your usurpery will be undone. You
will stand naked in the sun, exposed as the un-royal ones you
are. Fly specks. The shit left floating on the ocean's face after
the shipwreck. This time, I will be immortal because the dead
can never die. Cringing Set, when you slit my throat, I
ascended to heaven kissed seraphim once disguised as men,
long dead prophets,
ancient warriors born not from the race of Cain, slain
by the hands of those too dumb to know gods
when they met them. I drained three glasses from the river of
life and drank them. They burned me to bones. intertwined
my mind with the prime mover, shrink wrapped me in god
skin. This time I will fly. Oh, dead things
who dream yourselves alive, only the divine ones know the
things I know. A resurrected thing, I will be
the most glorious specter you have ever seen.
Made of mist. God kissed. Darkness tremble.
I am coming. This time I'm bullet proof.

Acknowledgements:

Many of these poems were not published in journals, as they were an ongoing love letter for a beloved individual, which I posted on my blog, tawniwaters.wordpress.com. However, I would like to thank the journals in which some of these poems appeared.

Rock & Sling
"Miss USA"
Quail Bell Magazine
"Hagseed Takes Manhattan"
Rathalla Review
"AWOL Icon: A Love Song Without Music"
Rathalla Review
"Overlooked"
Rathalla Review
"Outside the Chapel of Immaculate Conception"
Rathalla Review
"Kitsched"
Burlesque Press Variety Show
"Phenomenon"
Burlesque Press Variety Show
"Inanna's Imperative"

About the Author

Tawni Waters is the author of two novels, *Beauty of the Broken* (Simon & Schuster) and *The Long Ride Home* (Sourcebooks Fire), and a poetry collection, *Siren Song* (Burlesque Press). *Beauty of the Broken* was adapted for the stage and performed live and is now being adapted for the screen. Her writing has garnered multiple awards, including the prestigious ILA, and has been published in myriad journals, magazines, and anthologies, including *Best Travel Writing 2010* and *The Soul of a Great Traveler*. She teaches creative writing at various universities and writers conferences throughout the U.S., Europe, and Mexico. A professional wanderer, she lives on the road full time. This is her first collaboration with her daughter, illustrator Desiree Wade. Learn more at tawniwaters.com.

About the Artist

Desiree Wade wandered aimlessly until the age of 27, interpreting the world around her with a pen and paintbrush, until her mother asked if she'd like to illustrate her book. She lives in the space between this world and the next, reading, painting visions, and dancing with her cat, Artemis. Her debut graphic novel, *Heir Apparent,* is forthcoming. Her art can be found @seraphim.art on Instagram.

Lightning Source UK Ltd.
Milton Keynes UK
UKHW020645071019
351141UK00010B/129/P